FIRST AMERICANS
The Apache

CAROLYN CASEY

 **Marshall Cavendish**
Benchmark
New York

ACKNOWLEDGMENTS

Series consultant: Raymond Bial

Benchmark Books
Marshall Cavendish
99 White Plains Road
Tarrytown, New York 10591
www.marshallcavendish.us

Library of Congress Cataloging-in-Publication Data
Casey, Carolyn.
The Apache / by Carolyn Casey.
p. cm. -- (First Americans)
Summary: "Provides a general overview of the Apache people for young
readers. Covers history, daily life, and beliefs and contains recipe and
craft"--Provided by publisher.
Includes bibliographical references and index.
ISBN 0-7614-1894-6
1. Apache Indians--History--Juvenile literature. 2. Apache
Indians--Social life and customs--Juvenile literature. I. Title. II.
Series: First Americans Marshall Cavendish Benchmark
E99.A6C37 2005
979.004'9725--dc22
2005001141

On the cover: A young Apache girl in traditional dress at the Navajo Nation Fair in Shiprock, New Mexico.
Title page: Apache basket makers decorated their work with different shapes and figures of people and animals.

Photo Research by Joan Meisel

Cover photo: Marilyn "Angel" Wynn/Nativestock.com

The photographs in this book are used by permission and through the courtesy of *Corbis*: Edward S. Curtis, 8; Ben Wittick, 13; David G. Houser, 19, 23; Raymond Gehman, 30; Catherine Karnow, 40. *Getty Images*: Hulton Archive, 11, 14, 16. Marilyn "Angel" Wynn/Nativestock.com: 1, 4, 21, 22, 31, 32, 36, 38. *North Wind Picture Archive*: 10, 18. *Peter Arnold, Inc.*: Jeff Henry, 6; Martha Cooper, 28, 29. *The Philbrook Museum of Art*, Tulsa, Oklahoma: Allan Houser, Chiricahua Apache (1914-1994), *Fresh Trail Apache War Party*, 1952, watercolor on board, museum purchase 1952.10, 24; David Williams, *Apache Puberty Ceremony*, 1975, watercolor on board, museum purchase 1976.11.5, 26.

Map and illustrations by Christopher Santoro
Series design by Symon Chow

Printed in China
1 3 5 6 4 2

CONTENTS

1 · WHO ARE THE APACHE PEOPLE?

The land where the Apache lived covered a large area that contained high mountains, deep canyons, hot, dry deserts, and dense forests. It was a harsh land where wild animals wandered looking for food.

This land covered parts of present-day Colorado, Utah, Arizona, Texas, and New Mexico. Some Apache also lived in Mexico. The Apache Indians lived in these places long before the United States was formed.

The Apache were **nomadic**, which means they traveled from place to place instead of settling in farms and villages. They hunted deer, rabbits, turkeys, and other animals. The women gathered wild plants to use as food and materials for clothing and shelter. The Apache also were known for raiding other Indian camps, taking food, supplies, and horses.

The Apache made their home in a harsh land of mountains, valleys, deserts, and canyons.

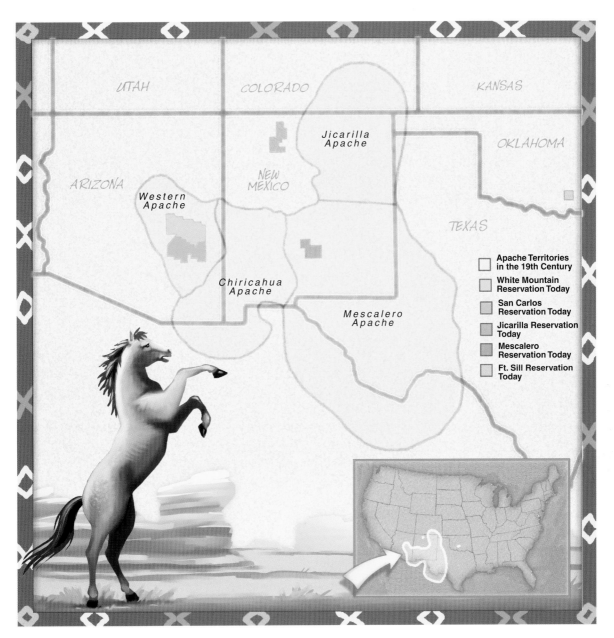

Apache lands once covered an area from Arizona to Texas and as far north as Colorado.

joined with other Native Americans to fight the Spanish settlers. The Apache attacked the villages, stealing horses and food. The settlers fought back, capturing the Apache and forcing them to become slaves. They also took Apache land.

The Apaches fought Spanish and Mexican settlers through the 1700s. Some Apache chose to live peacefully with the Spanish, but others continued to threaten anyone

An Apache ambushes a wagon train. The Apache tried for many years to keep different groups from taking over their lands.

who came onto their land.

Mexico won its independence from Spain in 1821 and took over New Mexico and other Apache lands. The Apache lived under Mexican rule until the United States declared war on Mexico in 1846. After the Mexican War, in 1848, the United States won ownership of most of the Southwest, including Apache territory.

This photograph of Geronimo with his band of warriors was taken in 1886.

Geronimo

One of the most famous Apaches was a warrior named Goyahkla or "One Who Yawns." When he was a young man in the 1850s, his tribe was traveling to a place in Mexico where they would be given blankets and cloth from the government. Goyahkla left the tribe at camp while he went to the trading post. A Mexican general and his men attacked the women and children at the camp and killed or captured them. Goyahkla's mother, wife, and three children were killed. For days Goyahkla refused to speak or eat.

During that time he had a vision that told him he could not be killed by guns. This vision encouraged him to fight the Mexicans. And that is what he did. He became a leader of his people and a warrior who kept the Apache from being taken captive and losing their land for nearly thirty years. He escaped from reservations several times, but was never allowed to return to his homeland. Goyahkla died on a reservation in 1909.

He became known as Geronimo, the name the Mexicans gave him. He stood out in history because he fought to protect the Apache and to help them keep their land.

An Apache family outside their home on the Jicarilla Reservation, about 1937.

For the next thirty years or so, the U.S. government fought the Apache. These battles were known as the Apache Wars. In the 1870s the Apache were defeated and forced to live on **reservations**—lands the U.S. government set aside for Native Americans to live on.

Life was very hard on the reservations. The Apache were given land that was too poor for farming and were forced to stay in one place. Many became sick. Their children were sent away to live in government schools where they were only allowed to speak English. Between 1900 and 1920, nearly one out of every four Apaches died.

2 · HOW THE APACHE LIVED

The harsh, dry land the Apache lived on could not support large groups of people. So the Apache lived in bands of just four or five families. Each family had a head man who made sure everyone did their jobs. Each band usually had a leader or chief.

The Apache family was centered around the mother. Mothers carried babies on **cradleboards** that were strapped to their backs. When a daughter married, she and her husband would stay with the daughter's band. The wife's grandmother was very respected in the family.

The Apache moved about every two weeks, so they had to create homes that were easy to take from place to place. Most Apache families lived in homes called **wickiups**. These were small, dome-shaped huts covered with brush or animal skins. It was the women's job to set up and take down the wickiup

The traditional Apache dwelling is called a wickiup. A mother and daughter working together could build a wickiup in just a few hours.

and to sweep the dirt floor clean.

The Apache women packed all their possessions in woven baskets each time they traveled. The baskets the women made could hold heavy loads. They hung the baskets across their back and shoulders. The baskets were made from different plants, reeds, and herbs—mainly yucca leaves, willow reeds, or juniper bark. Flowers from plants were used to make dyes

An Apache summer shelter called a shade.

for painting designs on the baskets.

Apache men wore **buckskin** pants, ponchos, and moccasins. Men usually wore their hair shoulder length with a headband tied across the forehead. Women wore buckskin skirts, ponchos, and moccasins. They also wore their hair long.

Food that was collected or killed was shared with the entire band. The Apache gathered desert plants, like the agave, to bake over hot rocks. They also ate pine nuts, walnuts, acorns, and

The Apache used large baskets to carry food and other items.

19

Apache Fry Bread

You will need:

  4 cups all-purpose flour
  $1/2$ teaspoon salt
  1 tablespoon baking powder
  $1 1/2$ cups warm water
  vegetable oil

Ask an adult for help.

1. Combine flour, salt, and baking powder in a large bowl. Add the water and stir until the dough forms a ball.

2. Put some flour on a clean countertop. Spread it around. Take the dough out of the bowl and place it on the countertop. Knead the dough until it is soft but not sticky.

3. Pull off pieces of dough, each about the size of a small peach. Shape into patties with floured hands. The patties should be about $1/2$ inch thick.

4. In a heavy skillet, heat the vegetable oil (about 1 inch deep). Fry the patties one at a time. Once the bottom is brown, flip the patty over with a spatula so it browns on both sides.

5. Drain bread on paper towels and serve warm with honey or jam.

cactus fruits. Some raised corn, beans, and other crops. The Apache hunted deer, jackrabbits, wild pigs, and even rats and lizards. Apaches who had horses hunted buffalo.

In preparation for winter, meat was dried, wild honey was stored, and a nutritious emergency food called **pemmican** was made. The women made pemmican by mixing ground acorns with dried meat and animal fat and rolling it into balls. All of these emergency foods were put into clay pots

The Apache started to wear cotton clothing after the arrival of Mexican settlers, but Apache men and women still wore traditional deerskin moccasins.

The Apache ate a variety of wild foods. Acorns were ground up and used to make different things like pemmican and acorn stew.

and hidden underground or in caves.

Children were expected to be tough and strong so they could survive. Every day—even in the winter—boys would wake up early and swim in a stream. Sometimes they were told to roll in the snow so they could get used to the cold. Girls also ran and swam to become strong.

Young boys were taught to be warriors. They learned how to be absolutely silent when they traveled and how to go without sleep all night

A Saguaro cactus towers over an agave plant in the Arizona desert. The Apache baked agave over hot rocks.

This painting by an Apache artist, called *Fresh Trail War Party*, shows a group of Apache warriors ready for battle.

while standing guard. Boys also learned how to send and read smoke signals. They began hunting with bows and arrows when they were eight or nine. By the time they were fifteen, boys were old enough to take part in raids and fighting.

Girls were taught the jobs of preparing food, weaving baskets, setting up the wickiup, and caring for babies. Preserving food was very important, and young girls of the Western Apache were often told the story of a young woman who saved the people during a time of starvation with her preserved food.

Traditionally, the Apache people believed that everything—people, animals, plants, and even the earth itself—was alive and had a spirit. The sun, moon, and sky were all spirits. The mountain spirits, called *Gan*, represented good power.

Certain animals, especially owls, bears, and coyotes, were believed to be bad spirits that brought sickness and bad luck. Healing ceremonies called upon the good power of the Gan to make sick people well again.

Shamans, or medicine men, were older men and women in the tribe who had special spiritual powers. They would lead ceremonies, help people understand dreams, and help heal the sick.

Pollen was used in many ceremonies. It represented life, fertility, beauty, and health. Newborn babies were sprinkled with pollen. Pollen is also used in the Apache girls' coming-of-age ritual. This celebration is called the Sunrise Ceremony.

The Sunrise Ceremony welcomes Apache girls into womanhood.

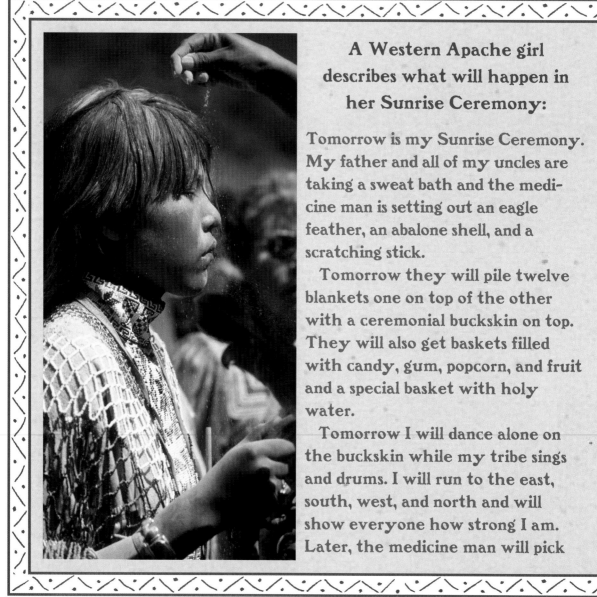

A Western Apache girl describes what will happen in her Sunrise Ceremony:

Tomorrow is my Sunrise Ceremony. My father and all of my uncles are taking a sweat bath and the medicine man is setting out an eagle feather, an abalone shell, and a scratching stick.

Tomorrow they will pile twelve blankets one on top of the other with a ceremonial buckskin on top. They will also get baskets filled with candy, gum, popcorn, and fruit and a special basket with holy water.

Tomorrow I will dance alone on the buckskin while my tribe sings and drums. I will run to the east, south, west, and north and will show everyone how strong I am. Later, the medicine man will pick up a basket filled with candy, corn kernels, acorns, and coins and pour it over my head. Everyone will gather round to scoop them up. When the ceremony is almost over, the medicine man and all the adults will bless me with holy pollen. When the ceremony ends, I will step off the buckskin and throw a blanket in each direction.

When everything is over I will have changed from a girl to a young woman.

Traditionally, girls married when they were fifteen to eighteen years old. Young men did not marry until they were between twenty to twenty-five years old because they had to prove their hunting and fighting skills before they were allowed to marry. Unlike some Native Americans, the Apache did not have a formal wedding ceremony. Usually the young man gave the young woman's family gifts of horses,

The Dance of the Mountain Gods is performed to thank the spirits for land, sky, water, and fire.

guns, and blankets. The bride's family gave some smaller gifts.

The Apache were very afraid of the ghosts of dead people. When a person died, the band members quickly buried the body or put it in a cave. They worried about diseases and about attracting the ghosts of the dead. Once someone had died, the band did not mention his or her

Corn pollen is used in many Apache ceremonies.

An Apache Crown Dancer performing the Mountain Spirit dance.

name because they did not want to anger the ghost.

Families usually buried or burned everything the dead person owned. After a death, the band moved to another camp.

Today the Apache continue to practice many of these sacred ceremonies. While most are now Christians, many have blended their Christian beliefs with their traditional Apache beliefs and rituals so they can honor all of their spirituality.

Apache Medicine Shield

When Apache men went into battle they wore headdresses with hawk and eagle feathers, and buckskin moccasins that helped make their footsteps silent. They sometimes fought with medicine shields, called *nas-ta-zhih*, that were made from stretched, dried animal hide. These shields were painted and decorated with feathers hanging from them. The Apache believed the medicine shields, usually made by war shamans, gave them spiritual protection.

Here is how to make a modern-day version of a medicine shield.

You will need:

- yarn
- scissors
- feathers
- construction paper
- felt-tipped pens
- heavyweight dinner-sized paper plate, like Chinet
- one-hole punch
- glue

1. Decorate the back of the paper plate with designs. Remember the Apache believed animals and plants had special powers. You might want to draw animals or cut out shapes with construction paper and glue them onto your plate.

2. Punch two holes near the top of the plate and six holes along the bottom.

3. Cut six pieces of yarn, each about 6 inches (15 cm) long and one piece about 18 inches (46 cm) long. Loop the longer piece through the top two holes and tie the ends together so you can hang the shield around your neck.

4. Take the shorter yarn pieces and thread each one through a hole and tie both ends to a feather. If you don't have any feathers, you can make them out of construction paper and punch a hole through the end.

4 · A CHANGING WORLD

In the year 2000 about 57,000 Apache people lived in the United States. There were 40,000 who were part Apache. Many of these people live on reservations in Arizona, New Mexico, and Oklahoma.

Today the Apache people still struggle with poverty. But new businesses are helping the Apache have a better way of life. They usually dress like other Americans, saving traditional clothes for special celebrations.

Driving through the Apache homeland, one might think the traditional way of life had been lost. The people live in modern houses, shop at supermarkets and malls, and work at regular jobs. But the Apache continue to speak their own language and preserve the old traditions.

Boys are still taught the old ways by their parents and

Three Apache girls participate at one of the many events held throughout the year where Native Americans celebrate their heritage.

shamans. They learn about the prayers, rituals, and plants that are used in healing ceremonies. Girls still celebrate the Sunrise Ceremony.

Many Apaches work in jobs such as farming, cattle and sheep ranching, and basket making. On the San Carlos Reservation, during the hot summer, women still hike into the hills to gather acorns.

Today, many Apache live on reservations like this one in northern Arizona.

Apache Language

Different Apache tribes speak slightly different dialects of the same language. Many of the words are the same. It is very important to the Apache people to preserve their native language. Tribal schools bring in elders to help teach children the Apache language and to help keep their traditions alive. Here are a few Apache words from the *Western Apache-English Dictionary*:

Apache word	Pronounced	English word
shash	*sh-ah-sh*	bear
ishkiin	*eesh-keen*	boy
ko'	*koh*	fire
it'een	*EET-ehn*	girl
oltag	*ohl-tahg*	school
aa	*ah*	yes

And Apaches are managing successful businesses. These businesses provide jobs to the growing number of educated Apache people. For example, the White Mountain Apache own and operate a very successful ski resort and casino. Other Apache tribes also have started tourism businesses with resorts, golf courses, and outdoor adventures.

The Apache have long been known as skilled horsemen. Today, many Apaches enjoy participating in rodeos.

Some of the money from these businesses is spent on improving the community. Office buildings, daycare centers, firehouses, and many other things have been paid for with money from Apache businesses.

The Apache people will continue to survive, and to prosper, in the modern world, while the next generation is taught about their ancient heritage.

· TIME LINE

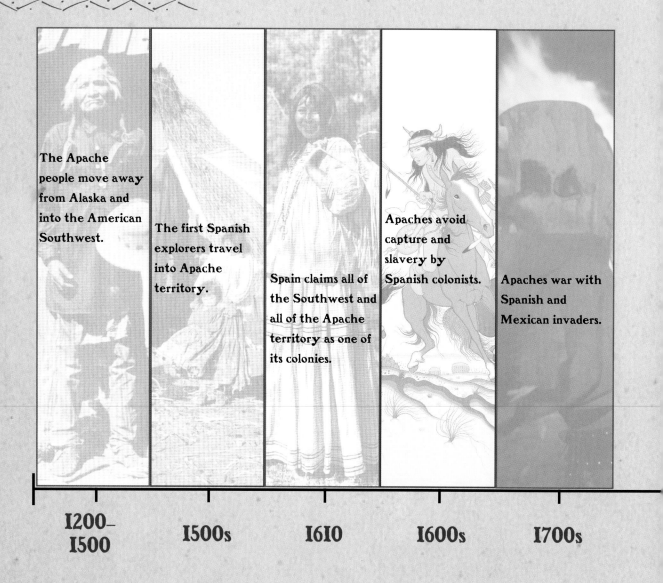

The Apache people move away from Alaska and into the American Southwest.

The first Spanish explorers travel into Apache territory.

Spain claims all of the Southwest and all of the Apache territory as one of its colonies.

Apaches avoid capture and slavery by Spanish colonists.

Apaches war with Spanish and Mexican invaders.

1200–1500 **1500s** **1610** **1600s** **1700s**

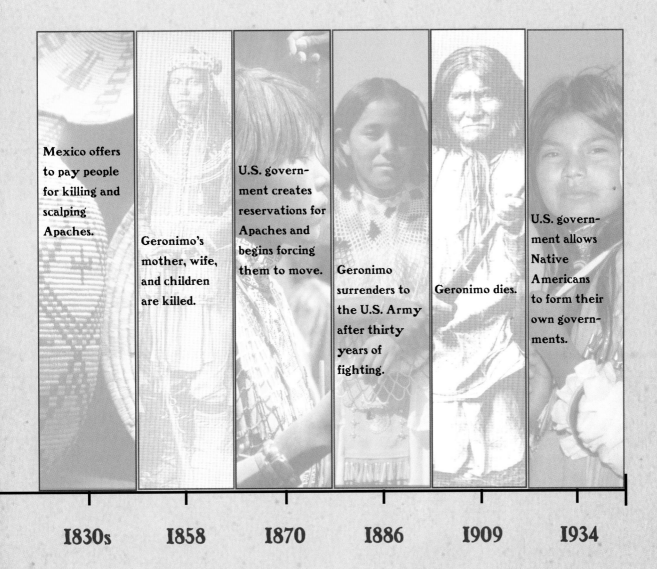

Mexico offers to pay people for killing and scalping Apaches.

Geronimo's mother, wife, and children are killed.

U.S. government creates reservations for Apaches and begins forcing them to move.

Geronimo surrenders to the U.S. Army after thirty years of fighting.

Geronimo dies.

U.S. government allows Native Americans to form their own governments.

1830s   1858   1870   1886   1909   1934

· GLOSSARY

buckskin: Leather made from the skin of a buck (male deer).

cradleboard: A wooden board that was strapped to a mother's back for her to carry her baby.

Ndee: (pronounced in-DAY) The Apache name for themselves, which means "the people."

nomadic: People who travel from place to place instead of settling in one location.

pemmican: A very nutritious food preserved for emergencies and winter. It is made of acorns mixed with buffalo jerky and fat, and rolled into balls.

reservations: A section of land set aside by the U.S. government for use by American Indians.

shaman: The medicine man or woman who uses magic and leads Apache religious ceremonies.

wickiup: Traditional Apache dwelling.

Books

Bial, Raymond. *The Apache*. New York: Marshall Cavendish Corp., 2001.

Doherty, Craig A. *The Apaches and the Navajo*. New York:Franklin Watts, 1989.

Holmas, Stig. *Son-of-Thunder*. Tucson, Arizona: Harbinger House, 1993.

Melody, Michael. *The Apache*. New York: Chelsea House, 1989.

Reedstrom, E. Lisle. *Apache Wars: An Illustrated Battle History*. New York: Sterling Publishing, 1990.

Schwarz, Melissa. *Geronimo, Apache Warrior*. New York: Chelsea House, 1992.

Web Sites

White Mountain Apache Tribe
www.wmat.nsn.us/

Yavapai Apache Tribe
www.yavapai-apache.org/

History of Apache and traditional stories and songs
www.indians.org/welker/apache.htm

Chiricahua and Mescalero Apache Stories
www.geocities.com/athens/delphi/2897/

About the Author

The Apache is writer Carolyn Casey's third nonfiction book for children. A former newspaper reporter, Casey now works in public relations for a port district in Washington state where she lives with her husband and sons.